D1124327

BY THOMAS K. ADAMSON

THE SEATTLE
SEAHAWKS
STORY

BELLWETHER MEDIA · MINNEAPOLIS, MN

TM

Are you ready to take it to the extreme? Torque books thrust you into the action-packed world of sports, vehicles, mystery, and adventure. These books may include dirt, smoke, fire, and chilling tales. **WARNING**: read at your own risk.

This edition first published in 2017 by Bellwether Media, Inc.

No part of this publication may be reproduced in whole or in part without written permission of the publisher. For information regarding permission, write to Bellwether Media, Inc., Attention: Permissions Department, 5357 Penn Avenue South, Minneapolis, MN 55419.

Library of Congress Cataloging-in-Publication Data

Names: Adamson, Thomas K., 1970-
Title: The Seattle Seahawks Story / by Thomas K. Adamson.
Description: Minneapolis, MN : Bellwether Media, Inc., 2017. | Series:
   Torque: NFL Teams | Includes index.
Identifiers: LCCN 2015043275 | ISBN 9781626173828 (hardcover : alk. paper)
Subjects: LCSH: Seattle Seahawks (Football team)–History–Juvenile literature.
Classification: LCC GV956.S4 A36 2017 | DDC 796.332/6409797772–dc23
LC record available at http://lccn.loc.gov/2015043275

Printed in the United States of America, North Mankato, MN.

TABLE OF CONTENTS

The Seattle Seahawks and Denver Broncos go head-to-head in **Super Bowl** 48. The Seahawks jump to an early lead.

Malcolm Smith

QUICK SCORE
The Seahawks scored a safety just 12 seconds into the game. It was the quickest score in Super Bowl history!

In the second quarter, the Broncos' **quarterback** takes a hit as he throws. The ball wobbles in the air. **Linebacker** Malcolm Smith grabs it for Seattle. He runs 69 yards for a touchdown!

Doug Baldwin

The Broncos finally score in the third quarter. But Seattle soon answers. Quarterback Russell Wilson throws to Doug Baldwin. The **wide receiver** ducks under defenders and dives into the end zone. Touchdown!

The final score is 43 to 8. The Seahawks win their first-ever National Football League (NFL) championship!

Russell Wilson

SCORING TERMS

END ZONE

the area at each end of a football field; a team scores by entering the opponent's end zone with the football.

EXTRA POINT

a score that occurs when a kicker kicks the ball between the opponent's goal posts after a touchdown is scored; 1 point.

FIELD GOAL

a score that occurs when a kicker kicks the ball between the opponent's goal posts; 3 points.

SAFETY

a score that occurs when a player on offense is tackled behind his own goal line; 2 points for defense.

TOUCHDOWN

a score that occurs when a team crosses into its opponent's end zone with the football; 6 points.

TWO-POINT CONVERSION

a score that occurs when a team crosses into its opponent's end zone with the football after scoring a touchdown; 2 points.

The Seahawks are in a region all on their own. No other NFL team is located in the **Pacific Northwest**.

The team is also special for having an official 12th player. Seattle's fans, called the 12s, cheer loud enough at home games to affect plays!

The Seahawks play their home games at CenturyLink Field in Seattle, Washington. The outdoor stadium has some cover. Its **canopies** protect most fans from the city's rain.

These canopies also magnify the crowd noise. In a 2011 game, the 12s caused a small earthquake in the stadium. Fans were cheering a huge touchdown run by Marshawn Lynch.

CENTURYLINK FIELD

Marshawn Lynch
January 8, 2011

SEATTLE,
WASHINGTON

N
W + E
S

CENTURYLINK FIELD

The NFL added two **expansion teams** for the 1976 season. The Seahawks were one of those teams.

The Seahawks play in the West **Division** of the National Football **Conference** (NFC). Their main **rival** is a California team, the San Francisco 49ers.

NFL DIVISIONS

 **AFC**

AFC NORTH

 BALTIMORE **RAVENS**

 CINCINNATI **BENGALS**

 CLEVELAND **BROWNS**

 PITTSBURGH **STEELERS**

AFC EAST

 BUFFALO **BILLS**

 MIAMI **DOLPHINS**

 NEW ENGLAND **PATRIOTS**

 NEW YORK **JETS**

AFC SOUTH

 HOUSTON **TEXANS**

 INDIANAPOLIS **COLTS**

JACKSONVILLE **JAGUARS**

TENNESSEE **TITANS**

AFC WEST

DENVER **BRONCOS**

 KANSAS CITY **CHIEFS**

 OAKLAND **RAIDERS**

 SAN DIEGO **CHARGERS**

NFC **NORTH**

 CHICAGO
BEARS

 DETROIT
LIONS

 GREEN BAY
PACKERS

 MINNESOTA
VIKINGS

NFC **EAST**

 DALLAS
COWBOYS

 NEW YORK
GIANTS

 PHILADELPHIA
EAGLES

 WASHINGTON
REDSKINS

NFC **SOUTH**

 ATLANTA
FALCONS

 CAROLINA
PANTHERS

NEW ORLEANS
SAINTS

 TAMPA BAY
BUCCANEERS

NFC **WEST**

 ARIZONA
CARDINALS

 LOS ANGELES
RAMS

 SAN FRANCISCO
49ERS

 SEATTLE
SEAHAWKS

The Seahawks struggled at the beginning. They only won two games during their first season. One victory was over the winless Tampa Bay Buccaneers.

1976 season

In the 1980s, the Seahawks won more and more. They made it to the **playoffs** four times. Their 1983 season almost ended with a Super Bowl appearance.

SUPER BOWL 40
FEBRUARY 5, 2006

The 1990s included only one playoff appearance. Since 2000, the Seahawks have had mostly strong seasons and played in multiple Super Bowls.

In Super Bowl 40, the team could not overpower the Pittsburgh Steelers. But Super Bowl 48 was a win! The next year, they just missed out on being repeat champions.

SUPER BOWL 48
FEBRUARY 2, 2014

SEAHAWKS TIMELINE

1974
Awarded to Seattle as an expansion NFL team

1976
Played first season in the NFL

1995
Celebrated the first Seahawk selection for the Pro Football Hall of Fame, wide receiver Steve Largent

1983
Made first playoff appearance, beating the Denver Broncos

 31 FINAL SCORE 7

2002
Played first home game in new stadium, later named CenturyLink Field

2006

Played in first Super Bowl, but lost to the Pittsburgh Steelers

10 FINAL SCORE **21**

2014

Won Super Bowl 48, beating the Denver Broncos

43 FINAL SCORE **8**

2012

Drafted star quarterback Russell Wilson

2015

Won the NFC Championship in overtime, beating the Green Bay Packers

28 FINAL SCORE **22**

Jim Zorn was an early star on the Seahawks. He was a tough **mobile** quarterback. Many of his passes were to wide receiver Steve Largent. When Largent left the NFL after the 1989 season, he held all the league's major receiving records.

Jim Zorn

Steve Largent

GUARD THE QUARTERBACK

Offensive tackle Walter Jones was a strong blocker. In 2004, he did not allow any sacks.

Quarterback Matt Hasselbeck became the Seahawks' all-time leading passer in the 2000s. He threw for 29,434 yards.

In both 2012 and 2013, **cornerback** Richard Sherman wowed with eight **interceptions**. His big defensive play in the playoffs for the 2013 season sent Seattle to Super Bowl 48.

His teammate Russell Wilson is the current face of the team. He is smart and calm under pressure. Defenses never know if he will run or pass.

TEAM GREATS

JIM ZORN
QUARTERBACK
1976-1984

STEVE LARGENT
WIDE RECEIVER
1976-1989

WALTER JONES
OFFENSIVE TACKLE
1997-2008

INTO THE END ZONE

In 2005, running back Shaun Alexander ran for an amazing 27 touchdowns!

MATT HASSELBECK
QUARTERBACK
2001-2010

MARSHAWN LYNCH
RUNNING BACK
2010-2015

RUSSELL WILSON
QUARTERBACK
2012-PRESENT

In 1984, the Seahawks retired jersey number 12 for fans. The team wanted to recognize them for their support. Today, many Seattle fans wear number 12 jerseys like uniforms.

At every home game, a flag is raised to honor the fans. The blue flag has a large number 12 on it.

The roar of the 12s makes communication on the field hard for opponents. It also stresses them out. They often **false start** or miss field goals.

Since 2005, the Seahawks have forced more false starts at their homes games than any other team. Their noisy, involved fans are to thank.

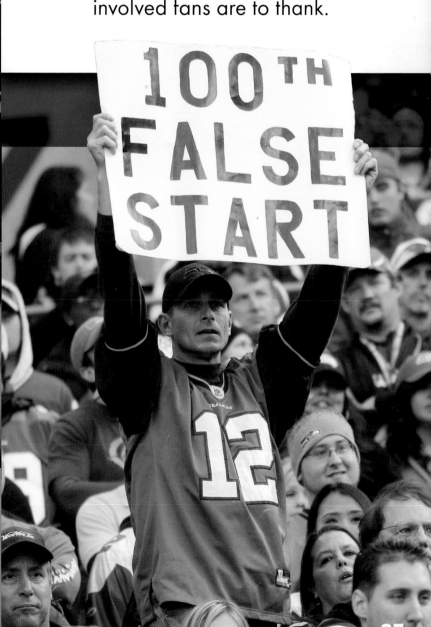

MORE ABOUT THE
SEAHAWKS

Team name:
Seattle Seahawks

Team name explained:
**Named after birds of
prey called ospreys;
ospreys are fish-hawks.**

Joined NFL: 1976

Conference: NFC

Division: West

**Main rivals: San Francisco 49ers,
Arizona Cardinals**

Hometown: Seattle, Washington

Training camp location: Virginia Mason Athletic Center, Renton, Washington

SEATTLE

WASHINGTON

N W + E S

Home stadium name: CenturyLink Field

Stadium opened: 2002

Seats in stadium: 67,000

Name for fan base: The 12s

Mascots: Blitz, Boom, Taima (live bird)

Logo: Tough-looking bird head, inspired by a mask used by the Kwakwaka'wakw tribe of the Pacific Northwest

Colors: Blue, green, gray

Blitz

GLOSSARY

canopies—hanging shelters or overhead covers

conference—a large grouping of sports teams that often play one another

cornerback—a player on defense whose main job is to stop wide receivers from catching passes; a cornerback is positioned outside of the linebackers.

division—a small grouping of sports teams that often play one another; usually there are several divisions of teams in a conference.

expansion teams—new teams added to a sports league

false start—to earn a penalty as a defender by moving across the line of scrimmage before the ball is snapped

interceptions—catches made by defensive players of passes thrown by the opposing team

linebacker—a player on defense whose main job is to make tackles and stop passes; a linebacker stands just behind the defensive linemen.

mobile—able to move around easily

Pacific Northwest—the region of the United States that includes Washington, Oregon, Idaho, and Montana

playoffs—the games played after the regular NFL season is over; playoff games determine which teams play in the Super Bowl.

quarterback—a player on offense whose main job is to throw and hand off the ball

rival—a long-standing opponent

Super Bowl—the championship game for the NFL

wide receiver—a player on offense whose main job is to catch passes from the quarterback

TO LEARN MORE

AT THE LIBRARY

Anderson, Jameson. *Russell Wilson*. Minneapolis, Minn.: ABDO Publishing Company, 2015.

Temple, Ramey. *Seattle Seahawks*. New York, N.Y.: AV2 by Weigl, 2015.

Whiting, Jim. *The Story of the Seattle Seahawks*. Mankato, Minn.: Creative Education, 2014.

ON THE WEB

Learning more about the Seattle Seahawks is as easy as 1, 2, 3.

1. Go to www.factsurfer.com.

2. Enter "Seattle Seahawks" into the search box.

3. Click the "Surf" button and you will see a list of related web sites.

With factsurfer.com, finding more information is just a click away.

INDEX

The images in this book are reproduced through the courtesy of: Corbis, front cover (large, small), pp. 9, 23 (middle); Tribune Content Agency LLC/ Alamy, pp. 4, 17, 19 (top right, bottom); Carlo Allegri/ Reuters/ Newscom, pp. 4-5; Jason Szenes/ EPA/ Newscom, pp. 6-7; Xinhua/ Alamy, p. 7; Ted S. Warren/ AP Images, pp. 8-9, 27; Mat Hayward, p. 10; Elaine Thompson/ AP Images, p. 11 (top); f11photo, pp. 11 (bottom), 18 (bottom); Cal Sport Media/ Alamy, pp. 12-13; Deposit Photos/ Glow Images, pp. 12-13 (logos), 18-19 (logos), 28-29 (logos); NFL Photos/ AP Images, pp. 14-15, 22 (left, middle); Kirthmon F. Dozier/ KRT/ Newscom, pp. 16-17; David Durochik/ AP Images, p. 18 (top); Rhona Wise/ EPA/ Newscom, p. 19 (top left); Al Messerschmidt/ AP Images, p. 20 (left); Gary Stewart/ AP Images, p. 20 (right); John Anderson/ UPI/ Newscom, p. 21; Les Walker/ Getty Images, pp. 22-23; Jim Bryant/ UPI/ Newscom, pp. 22 (right), 24-25, 28; Paul Spinelli/ AP Images, p. 23 (left); Greg Trott/ AP Images, p. 23 (right); David Gonzales/ Icon SMI/ Newscom, p. 25; Joshua Weisberg/ Icon Sportswire/ Newscom, pp. 26-27; Jim Corwin/ Alamy, p. 29 (stadium); Scott Boehm/ AP Images, p. 29 (mascot); Eric Bakke/ AP Images, p. 29 (bird).